TOMATOES

Here is a collection of innovative recipes for every kind of tomato, from the classic red, to the charming cherry, to the green and yellow varieties. The classics are included: "Fresh Tomato Juice", "Cream of Tomato Soup" and "Gazpacho", but here, too, are a variety of unusual, succulent dishes such as "Scallop Seviche with Tomatoes" (a first course), "Tomato Quiche" (a main dish), "Tomato Sherbet" (a fine refresher) and "Green Tomato Marmalade" (an unusual condiment).

secrets of vegetable cooking

. . . is a series of attractive, low-priced cookbooks, each concerned with a specific vegetable and, most important, each containing a collection of more than 50 distinctive and delicious recipes for the broadest range of vegetable dishes. A special treat—the soup to nuts of vegetable cookery.

Inez M. Krech, author of the entire series, is well known as a writer (she was the co-author of "Naturally Italian") and as the editor of more than 200 cookbooks. She lives in New Jersey.

secrets of vegetable cooking

Inquiries should be addressed to
Crown Publishers, Inc., One Park Avenue, New York, New York 10016

Printed in the United States of America

Published simultaneously in
Canada by General Publishing Company Limited

Library of Congress Cataloging in Publication Data

Krech, Inez M.
  Tomatoes.

  (Secrets of vegetable cooking)
  1. Cookery (Tomatoes) I. Title. II. Series: Krech,
Inez M. Secrets of vegetable cooking.
TX803.T6K73 1981   641.6'5642   81-5550
ISBN 0-517-54447-4   AACR2

10 9 8 7 6 5 4 3 2 1
First edition

DESIGN AND COVER PHOTOGRAPH BY ALBERT SQUILLACE

TOMATOES

by inez m. krech

primavera books ❧ crown publishers, inc. / new york

Introduction

Tomatoes, American natives, are one of our most popular vegetables, second to the potato in popularity in the United States. However, a tomato is not really a vegetable, but a fruit, botanically a berry with a seed formation related to that of the grape. This popularity began only about 100 years ago. Before that tomatoes were generally considered poisonous and were raised as ornamental plants. Since then hundreds of varieties have been developed, some for special uses.

Tomatoes are for sale all year long, but the best are those that ripen in your own area in their proper season—July through September, with some variation according to latitude.

Tomatoes are a good source of vitamin C, but it takes 8 ounces of tomato juice to equal the C in 4 ounces of orange juice. An average market tomato of 5 to 6 ounces (3 to a pound) will provide 35 calories, with 34 milligrams of vitamin C, about 350 milligrams of potassium and about 1350 international units of vitamin A, plus other vitamins, minerals and amino acids. Cooking tomatoes causes the loss of at least a third of the vitamins, but enough remains to make cooked or canned tomatoes a good source of nutrients. Even green tomatoes have a good amount of potassium and vitamins A and C.

Growing your own tomatoes will give you the chance to gather the fruits when they have completely ripened on the vine. No commercial tomato is allowed to remain so long on the plant, for it would then be subject to bruising in transit and would spoil. Also, varieties of tomatoes developed for commercial use have been bred with thick skins to withstand machine picking and to last long in trucking and storage. You can grow thin-skinned tomatoes, also several varieties for different uses. Only a small space is needed for a good crop. Be sure to choose plants good for your climate. You will need to provide rich soil and ample sun for best results. County or state agricultural agencies can help with advice, and there are many publications on gardening available from the U.S. Department of Agriculture. You can send away for these; or, if you live in a community with a library that serves as a government repository, you may be able to find these leaflets there.

In addition to standard varieties, there are tomatoes for early, midseason and late production. Also there are delicious yellow tomatoes, round, plum-shaped, and cherry size. There is even a green tomato, ripe when green. (Most green tomatoes are red tomatoes that have not ripened; these should be gathered before frost. There are several recipes here for these.) You can even find some that are more orange than red; one species of this color has outstanding content of vitamin A, or carotene.

A special tomato ideal for making tomato paste was developed from the Mediterranean plum tomato, but all plum tomatoes are good for cooking. The so-called cherry tomatoes come in several sizes. Some are actually cherry-size, but others are closer to the size of a blue plum, only rounder. Some tomatoes are less acid, others very acid.

When buying tomatoes retail, one seldom finds much information on variety or flavor, but you can choose the size that is suitable for your use. If you are planning to make lots of juice or sauce for canning or freezing, it is better to look for local tomatoes not raised for shipping; they may have been picked when nearly ripe and will have better flavor. Even when buying only a pound or two for immediate use, always take advantage of the local crop. Usually markets will label local tomatoes.

Tomatoes from your own garden, warmed by the sun, have a delicious spicy odor. The flavor is more delicious at room temperature. If you do not plan to use them at once, refrigerate fully ripe fruits, but bring them to room temperature again before serving.

If the tomatoes you buy are not fully ripe, do not refrigerate them, but place in a single layer, not touching, on a shelf or plate away from direct sunlight. Refrigerated unripe tomatoes become watery and are more likely to decay. The process of ripening has started within these fruits and they may become redder, but they will not become better. Vine-ripened tomatoes have twice as much vitamin C as hothouse tomatoes and much more than those picked while still somewhat green.

Do not wash tomatoes until you are ready to use them. However, it is important to remove any soil or leaves that may adhere. Use a dry cloth to rub off any soil; it may contain insects or mold spores which could start spoilage.

When the end of the season comes and you have masses of unripe tomatoes at hand, gather them all, gently rub off any soil, and arrange them in a single layer on trays or shelves. If you know you will not use them within a few weeks, wrap each one in newspaper and store in a cool area. Check the packages every week; some will never ripen, but will decay; discard those promptly to protect the rest. Following this procedure, I have had red tomatoes till the end of the year. If you do not have room for this storage, just cook the green tomatoes as if they were red; they will be different, but still good.

To Peel Tomatoes

Vine-ripened tomatoes are easy to peel; start at the blossom end and the skin will come off like a glove. When you reach the core, remove it.

Other tomatoes should be blanched. Bring a large pot of water to a boil and drop in a few tomatoes at a time. Leave them in the boiling water for 1 minute, then with a skimmer transfer to a bowl of cold water to prevent softening of the flesh. Peel—at this point it is simple.

The alternative method of spearing a tomato on a steel fork and turning it over a gas flame is not recommended. Too much juice can be lost that way, also the flesh of the tomato starts to cook and soften. The stove usually gets messed up too.

When should tomatoes be peeled? Generally whenever they are to be cooked, unless they will be put through a sieve or food mill after cooking. When tomato skins are cooked, they develop a texture like pieces or threads of silk, very tough and not really digestible. Any tomato dish becomes more elegant if the skins are removed. An exception: tomatoes that are to be stuffed and baked keep their shape better if the peel is left on. If you are working with cherry tomatoes to be stuffed for cold appetizers, peel or not as you choose, but for lots of these little fruits it will take time.

Unripe green tomatoes have very thin skins, so these are not usually peeled for any recipe.

To Remove Seeds

Split tomatoes and gently press the halves. This is easier with plum tomatoes. To save all the juices, do this over a strainer set in a bowl. To remove all seeds, tomatoes raw or cooked can be put through a food mill. Seeds can add bitterness to a dish, especially one that is cooked for a long time.

Preserving Tomatoes

Tomatoes can be dried, canned or frozen. To dry them, blanch, peel and core them, then cut into thin wedges or slices. Arrange the pieces in a single layer on drying racks or trays. (You can concoct your own racks, but they are not expensive to buy.) Put them in an oven heated to about 140°F. Leave the oven door slightly ajar to provide adequate ventilation. When the pieces are brittle, in about 12 hours, remove them from heat. Store in glass or plastic containers.

To use these for cooking, measure 1 cup pieces into a saucepan and add 1 cup boiling water. If the water is all absorbed in less than 1 hour, add more water, 1/4 cup at a time. Set rehydrated tomatoes over very low heat and simmer, stirring often, until tender. You may need to add a little more water during cooking.

To freeze uncooked tomatoes, wash them thoroughly, quarter them, and pack them in plastic freezer containers, leaving 1/2 inch of headspace. When you plan to use them, thaw them in the refrigerator overnight and put them through a food mill next day. Use for cooked dishes. Or they can be blanched and peeled before freezing.

Juice, purée, sauces and plain stewed tomatoes can be frozen. Use rigid plastic containers or glass jars. Leave 1 inch of headspace. Cool the containers, then put them in the freezer. When solidly frozen, seal and label. When you plan to use them, thaw in refrigerator overnight.

Whole small tomatoes can be frozen in plastic bags, but frozen tomatoes do not keep the texture of fresh tomatoes (they are only good for cooking) so it is easier to freeze them quartered or already cooked in some way. Whole fruits take up a lot of freezer space.

Canning is the old-fashioned method, and it is still good for tomatoes since the natural acid helps in preservation. But it is much more work than freezing. Nowadays such good commercially canned tomatoes are available that it is more economical to use these, if you count time and effort as a factor. Also the peeled plum tomatoes (pelati) make excellent winter sauces.

But if you plan to preserve tomatoes by canning, it is advisable that you follow the detailed instructions available from the manufacturer of the canning equipment or from the many excellent books available on the subject.

Unless you have a good source of tomatoes that can be gathered after ripening, do not plan to can plain tomatoes. Market tomatoes are too expensive and not flavorful enough for the effort. Canning small amounts of your own special sauce, juice or purée is more practical, but freezing is the simplest if you have adequate freezer space and live in an area that is not subject to multiple power failures.

A Note to Cooks

Some of the recipes call for the use of a blender or food processor. If you lack these appliances, do not discard the recipes. Any food can be sliced, chopped or minced with a chef's knife on a chopping board. A mortar and pestle can be used for grating, and there are inexpensive hand-operated utensils for shredding. The best tool for puréeing is the hand-operated food mill, available in several sizes.

Unsalted butter and olive oil were used in testing recipes. If it matters to the recipe, the ingredient list will specify "unsalted butter"; otherwise use what you prefer, but remember to adjust salt. If butter is prohibited, use margarine instead. Any vegetable oil or polyunsaturated oil can be substituted for olive, but the taste will be slightly different.

All recipes use relatively low amounts of salt and very little sugar; if you prefer more or less, adjust to taste. If either is prohibited, simply omit. You may want to adjust flavor with a little lemon juice or an additional pinch of herb if salt is omitted. If fructose is permitted, use that in place of cane sugar.

■ Ingredients are listed in **bold** type when they are first mentioned in the instructions and thereafter whenever it seems helpful in following the directions.

Fresh Tomato Juice

preparation time: 15 minutes
cooking time: 12 to 20 minutes
makes about 3 pints

4 pounds fully ripe tomatoes
1 tablespoon minced onion
3 fresh basil leaves
2 peppercorns, crushed
1 teaspoon salt
lemon slices or tiny leafy celery ribs
celery salt

1. Wash **tomatoes,** remove cores, and cut the fruits into quarters, or smaller chunks if they are large fruits. Put them in a stainless-steel or enamelware kettle. Add **onion, basil, peppercorns** and **salt.**

2. Mash enough tomatoes to release some juice in the bottom of the kettle, to prevent burning. Simmer the mixture over low heat, stirring often and mashing as tomatoes begin to soften, until you have a juicy mush.

3. Put the mixture, part at a time, through a food mill. If you want a thinner juice, put the milled purée through a fine strainer. Add more **salt** to your taste. Transfer the juice to glass jars and chill.

4. Serve cold in glasses, garnished with a **lemon slice** or a **celery rib,** and sprinkled with **celery salt.** Or heat and serve in bouillon cups with lemon slices.

variations: Instead of basil, use 1 bay leaf. Omit peppercorns, and instead use the crushed seeds of 2 cloves. Add 1 tiny garlic clove, put through a press.

Yellow Tomato Juice: If you are lucky enough to have 4 pounds of yellow tomatoes, these make a delicious juice. Omit basil and peppercorns. Season the finished juice carefully; it is less acid and will need less salt. Garnish with watercress leaves. For an unusual predinner drink, try mixing it half and half with apricot nectar.

Tomato Juice for Canning or Freezing

preparation time: 45 minutes
cooking time: 20 minutes, plus
15 minutes for processing
makes about 7 pints

10 pounds fully ripe tomatoes
1 tablespoon salt

1. Wash **tomatoes,** core them, and cut into quarters or smaller chunks if they are large fruits. Put them in a large stainless-steel or enamelware kettle. If you do not have one large enough, do this in several batches.

2. Mash enough tomatoes to release some juice in the bottom of the kettle, to prevent burning. Simmer tomatoes over low heat, stirring and mashing often, for about 20 minutes, or until tomatoes are reduced to a juicy mush.

3. Put them, part at a time, through a food mill. Wash the kettle. Return all the juice to the kettle and stir in the **salt.** Bring juice to a boil. Then pour or ladle it into sterilized 1-pint preserving jars. Seal them following the directions for your kind of jar.

4. Set the jars on a rack in a preserving kettle and pour in water to reach just below the caps. Bring to a boil and boil for 15 minutes. Lift out the jars with jar grippers and set them on a wooden board or rack to cool.

5. If you plan to freeze the finished juice, add salt and bring juice to a boil as in Step 3. Pour or ladle the juice into 1-pint freezer containers, allowing 1 inch of headspace, and cool in the refrigerator, then freeze. As soon as the juice is frozen, seal the lids well and overwrap with a sheet of clear plastic. Label.

6. Season or flavor juice to be canned or frozen when you are ready to serve it. Frozen juice will separate on thawing. Just shake well before serving.

note: Old-fashioned canning kettles have racks that hold 7 jars, either pints or quarts. If you have room to work with a double amount of tomatoes, you can use 1-quart jars. There are smaller kettles available that hold 4 jars. Adjust the amounts to the equipment you will work with.

Tomato and Mozzarella Salad

preparation time: 10 minutes
serves 4

8 ripe plum tomatoes, about 1 pound
1 pound whole-milk mozzarella cheese
4 fresh basil leaves
4 large parsley sprigs
1 lemon
salt and pepper
1 tablespoon olive oil
4 teaspoons snipped fresh chives

1. Blanch and peel **tomatoes,** core them, and cut them at an angle into oval slices. Cut the **cheese** into thin slices of the same shape.
2. Wash and dry **basil** and **parsley** and drop into the bowl of a food processor fitted with the steel blade. Peel the yellow rind (zest) from the **lemon** and drop the pieces into the processor. Chop the mixture.
3. Squeeze the juice from the **lemon.** Arrange **tomato** and **cheese slices** alternately on 4 salad plates. Sprinkle **lemon juice** over them, season with **salt,** and grind fresh **pepper** over all. Divide **herb** and **lemon-rind** mixture among the salads.
4. Flick tiny droplets of **oil** on the salads, and finish with 1 teaspoon **chives** on each plate. Serve as a first course.

Cherry Tomatoes Stuffed with Cheese

preparation time: 10 minutes
serves 6 to 8

24 cherry tomatoes, each about 1-1/4 inches across
3 ounces cream cheese
1-1/2 ounces Roquefort or other blue cheese
3 tablespoons minced parsley
3 tablespoons dairy sour cream
24 tiny mint leaves

1. Wash and dry **tomatoes.** With a sharp knife cut a slice off the stem end. Use the small end of a melon-ball scoop to empty the tomatoes (the pulp is not used in the recipe—set it aside for sauce or soup). Set scooped-out tomatoes upside down to drain.
2. Mix **cheeses, parsley** and **sour cream** and whip with a fork.
3. Fill each **tomato** with about 1 teaspoon of the mixture. Press a **mint leaf** in the top of each one. Serve with other cocktail foods.

Cherry Tomatoes Stuffed with Chicken

preparation time: 10 minutes
cooking time: 10 minutes to
     poach chicken
serves 6 to 8

24 cherry tomatoes, each about 1-1/4 inches across
3 ounces poached chicken breast
2 tablespoons minced green pepper
1 shallot, minced
2 tablespoons mayonnaise
1/2 teaspoon celery salt
salt and pepper
24 watercress leaves or tiny parsley sprigs

1. Wash and dry **tomatoes.** With a sharp knife cut a slice off the stem end. Use the small end of a melon-ball scoop to empty the tomatoes, and scoop the pulp into a strainer set over a bowl. Set scooped-out tomatoes upside down to drain.
2. With a wooden spoon press the juice and pulp through the sieve; discard seeds. Set the sieved tomato aside.
3. Mince the **chicken** and mix in **green pepper, shallot, mayonnaise** and **celery salt.** Season with **salt** and **pepper** to taste. Add 1 to 2 tablespoons of **sieved tomato** to the chicken mixture; it should not be soupy; add just enough to lighten the mixture. Whip with a fork to mix well.
4. Fill each **tomato** with about 1 teaspoon of the **chicken mixture.** Press a **watercress leaf** or **parsley sprig** into the top of each one. Serve with other cocktail foods, or as a garnish on a salad platter.

variation: Instead of chicken, use tuna or boneless roast veal or turkey.

Scallop Seviche with Tomatoes

preparation time: 10 to 15 minutes, plus 24 hours for marinating
serves 8 as a first course

1-1/2 pounds sea scallops
6 limes
6 shallots
3 fresh hot red peppers
8 black peppercorns
8 to 10 ripe plum tomatoes
2 tablespoons olive oil
16 leaves of Bibb lettuce
8 teaspoons minced parsley

1. Put **scallops** in a colander and spray them with cold water. Roll in paper towels to dry. Cut each large scallop into 2 or 3 slices, making round discs. Put the slices in a pottery or glass container.

2. Squeeze juice from **limes.** Peel **shallots** and slice them. Wearing rubber or plastic gloves, slit **hot peppers** and rinse out seeds. Discard stems and ribs. Cut peppers into thin slices. Crush **peppercorns.**

3. Sprinkle **lime juice** over **scallops** and scatter **shallot slices, pepper slices** and **peppercorns** over them. If the container is deep, add these ingredients in layers of scallops. Cover and refrigerate for 24 hours. If lime juice does not cover scallops, turn them once or twice during marinating so all are "cooked" by the acid of the lime juice.

4. Just before serving, wash and core **tomatoes.** Chop them and put them in a mixing bowl. With a skimmer, transfer **scallops** to the same bowl and add **olive oil.** Gently toss to mix. Add as much of the lime juice **marinade** as needed to flavor the mixture.

5. Line 8 coquilles (scallop shells) or plates with 2 **lettuce leaves** and divide the seviche among them. Sprinkle 1 teaspoon **parsley** over each one. Serve as a first course.

Tomato and Cheese Canapés

preparation time: 20 minutes
cooking time: about 8 minutes
makes 30 canapés, about 10
servings

1 pound firm white bread or oatmeal bread, sliced
2 ounces unsalted butter
10 round tomatoes, 2 inches across, or 7 or 8 large plum tomatoes, about 3
    ounces each
12 ounces Vermont Cheddar, Jarlsberg, or Havarti cheese
2 ounces blue cheese
1/2 cup mayonnaise
30 watercress leaves

1. Use a 2-inch round cutter to make 2 rounds of bread from each **bread slice;** you should have 30 rounds. Let **butter** soften at room temperature. Put the rounds on a baking sheet and slide under a preheated broiler for a minute or two. The rounds should be barely golden. Butter each one on the toasted side, using less than 1/2 teaspoon butter per round.
2. Blanch and peel **tomatoes.** Cut them across to make 3/8-inch slices from the middle; you can make about 3 slices from the round tomatoes, 4 or 5 from large plum tomatoes. The rest of the tomatoes can be used for another recipe.
3. Cut 30 round slices from the Cheddar, Jarlsberg or Havarti **cheese.** The kind you use depends on your taste. Vermont Cheddar is pungent, Jarlsberg less strong, Havarti mild and buttery. Arrange 1 **cheese slice** on each **toast round** and top with 1 **tomato slice.**
4. Crumble **blue cheese** into the **mayonnaise** and spread about 1 teaspoon of the mixture on each tomato.
5. When ready to serve, place on the baking sheet again and slide under the broiler. Broil for a few minutes only, until topping is bubbly and starting to brown. Add 1 **watercress leaf** to each canapé and serve at once.

Tomato Sherbet

preparation time: 15 minutes, plus 4 hours for freezing cooking time: 30 minutes serves 6 to 8

2 pounds ripe tomatoes
2 shallots
1 celery rib with leaves
salt
2 teaspoons sugar
2 cloves
1 cinnamon stick
1 strip of orange rind
2 egg whites
juice of 1 lemon
1/2 cup sour cream
6 to 8 mint leaves

1. Wash and core **tomatoes,** chop them, and drop them into a stainless-steel or enamelware saucepan. Peel and mince **shallots** and add to tomatoes, along with the **celery rib,** 1 teaspoon **salt,** the **sugar,** the crushed heads of the **cloves** (do not use the stems), the **cinnamon stick** broken into small pieces, and the **orange rind.** Bring to a boil, then simmer over very low heat until tomatoes are very soft, about 30 minutes.
2. Discard **cinnamon stick pieces, orange rind** and **celery.** Put everything else through a food mill, then force through a fine sieve. Taste, and add more **salt** if needed.
3. Pour into metal ice-cube trays and freeze for 1 hour. Beat **egg whites** with **lemon juice** and a pinch of **salt** until stiff but not dry. Scrape frozen sherbet into a cold bowl, beat with a rotary beater until smooth, then fold in **egg whites.**
4. Return to freezer and freeze for 3 hours, or until firm. Serve as a first course, garnished with **sour cream** and **mint leaves,** or as a "refresher" after the main course of a heavy dinner.

Tomato Soup Florentine

preparation time: 10 to 15
minutes
cooking time: 25 minutes
serves 6 to 8

2 pounds ripe tomatoes
2 large leeks
1 onion, 3 ounces
1 tablespoon olive oil
1 ounce butter
pinch of grated mace
4 cups chicken stock or vegetable broth
salt
20 spinach leaves
2 ounces tiny shell pasta or stellette

1. Wash **tomatoes,** remove cores, and chop. (No need to peel at this stage.) Wash **leeks,** cut into crosswise slices, and wash again. Peel and chop **onion.**
2. Heat **oil** and **butter** in a soup kettle and sauté **leeks** and **onion** until golden and translucent. Stir in **mace,** then the **chopped tomatoes.** Cook over low heat until tomatoes are soft.
3. Add **stock** or broth and continue to cook until tomatoes are dissolved in stock.
4. Put the mixture, part at a time, through a food mill. Wash out the soup kettle. Return soup to the kettle, and season with **salt** to taste.
5. Wash **spinach leaves** and pull off the stems. Put leaves in a saucepan and pour in enough boiling water to cover. Let spinach steep for 5 minutes, then drain, rinse with cold water, and drain again. Press to extract all water, then chop **spinach.**
6. Bring 2 quarts water to a boil, add 2 teaspoons **salt,** and drop in the **pasta.** Cook shells for 5 minutes, stellette for 2 or 3 minutes. Drain pasta.
7. Bring **tomato broth** to a boil, stir in **chopped spinach** and drained **pasta,** and serve at once. The tomato broth, spinach and pasta can all be prepared a day ahead, to be combined at the last minute. An excellent company soup.

variation: In winter this can be made with canned peeled plum tomatoes. Use two 20-ounce cans, including all the juice. You may prefer to omit mace if tomatoes are packed with basil. Instead add a pinch or so of dried basil.

Cream of Tomato Soup

1. Make **Tomato Soup Florentine,** following Steps 1 and 2. Add only 3 cups stock or broth, and continue with the recipe through Steps 3 and 4.
2. Combine 1 cup heavy **sweet cream** and 1 cup dairy **sour cream** and stir into the strained tomato mixture. Heat to just below a simmer. If the acid in tomatoes causes the soup to curdle, mix it with a rotary egg beater, or whirl in a blender until smooth.
3. Sprinkle each serving with snipped fresh **chives** or **watercress leaves.**

Chilled Cream of Tomato Soup

1. Follow Step 1 for **Cream of Tomato Soup.** Stir in 1 cup **light cream,** beat with a whisk to combine well, and chill for several hours or overnight.
2. Peel 1 small **cucumber.** Cut half of it into chunks and put in a blender or food processor with 3/4 cup **heavy cream.** Blend or process to a smooth purée. Mix into the chilled soup.
3. Cut remaining **cucumber** into slices and sprinkle them with chopped **parsley.** Float 2 slices on each serving of soup.

Gazpacho

preparation time: 20 minutes, plus 3 hours for chilling
serves 6 to 8

3 pounds fresh tomatoes
3 shallots
2 cucumbers
1/4 cup olive oil
1/4 cup fresh lemon juice
salt and pepper
Tabasco
1 Bermuda onion, 8 ounces
2 green peppers
1 cup toasted seasoned croutons

1. Blanch and peel **tomatoes,** core them, and cut into chunks. Drop into the bowl of a food processor fitted with the steel blade and chop tomatoes, about 2 cups at a time. Peel **shallots** and chop with the last batch of tomatoes. No need to wash the bowl or blade.

2. Push the whole mixture through a food mill to get rid of seeds, then turn into a large mixing bowl.

3. Peel 1 **cucumber,** halve it lengthwise, and scoop out any mature seeds. Cut cucumber into chunks and drop into the processor bowl. Add **olive oil** and **lemon juice** and process to chop cucumber and mix well. Stir into the **tomato purée,** season with **salt** and freshly ground **pepper** to taste, and add a few drops of **Tabasco.** Mix well, then cover and refrigerate for several hours.

4. Have ready 4 matching serving bowls with ladles. Peel and chop Bermuda **onion** and put the dice in one of the bowls. Peel the second **cucumber,** halve it, remove mature seeds, and chop; put these dice in a second bowl.

5. Char **green peppers** in oven or broiler and remove skins. Discard stems, ribs and seeds. Chop peppers and add to the third bowl. Finally put **croutons** in the fourth bowl.

6. At serving time, stir soup well and ladle into bouillon cups or small bowls. Each person adds the garnishes to the soup to his own taste.

variation: In an emergency this soup can be made with tomato juice, fresh or canned. Other garnishes can be added or substituted.

Provençal Shellfish Soup

preparation time: 20 minutes
cooking time: 15 to 20 minutes
serves 6

1 pound small clams
1 pound mussels
1 cup white wine
1 pound small squids
1/4 cup olive oil
3 garlic cloves
1/4 pound small white onions
1-1/2 pounds ripe tomatoes
2 cups fish stock
salt and pepper
few drops of anise-flavored liqueur (Pernod, etc.)
1/4 cup chopped fresh fennel

1. Scrub **clams** and **mussels.** Pour the **wine** and an equal amount of **water** into a steamer and steam **clams** until they open. Set clams aside and discard shells. Steam **mussels** in the same pot until they open. Discard any unopened mussels. Set mussels aside and discard shells. Filter the steaming liquid into a clean container.

2. Dress the **squids.** Separate head and tentacles from the body and discard head. Remove the rudimentary shell. Peel off the purple skin. Cut the squids into rings, rinse, and set aside.

3. Heat **olive oil** in a soup kettle. Peel **garlic** and push through a press into the oil. Peel and chop **onions** and add to garlic. Simmer over low heat until golden.

4. Meanwhile blanch and peel **tomatoes.** Chop them and add to the kettle. Simmer until tomatoes are almost reduced to a purée. Pour in **fish stock** and the filtered shellfish steaming liquid. Season with **salt** and **pepper** to taste. Bring to a boil.

5. Drop in the **squid** rings, simmer for 2 minutes, then drop in **clams** and **mussels** and leave at a simmer only until soup is hot. Stir in the anise-flavored **liqueur.** Garnish with chopped **fennel.**

6. Accompany with French bread croutons, rubbed with garlic and sautéed in olive oil.

variations: To make a more substantial soup, add 1 pound filleted fresh fish (red mullet, lotte, sea bass, etc.), cut into thin strips. Simmer for 4 minutes before adding squids. When good fresh tomatoes are lacking, use 3 or 4 cups canned plum tomatoes and add a pinch of sugar.

Broiled Tomatoes

preparation time: 5 minutes
cooking time: 5 to 6 minutes
serves 6

6 firm ripe tomatoes, about 6 ounces each
1 ounce Parmesan cheese
1/2 cup soft fresh bread crumbs
2 tablespoons minced parsley
1 teaspoon crumbled dried orégano
olive oil

1. Wash **tomatoes;** carefully cut out just the cores, leaving the surrounding flesh intact. Cut tomatoes into crosswise halves and place them, cut side down, on a cake rack to drain a little.
2. Grate the **cheese** and mix it with **crumbs, parsley** and **orégano.** Set **tomatoes** cut side up and divide the mixture among them. Set them on an oiled broiler pan. Flick a few drops of **olive oil** on each half.
3. Broil **tomatoes** for 5 to 6 minutes, until the topping is golden. Serve 2 halves as a vegetable, or 1 half as a garnish to fish, veal or chicken.

Braised Tomatoes

preparation time: 10 minutes
cooking time: 20 minutes
serves 4 to 6

8 small round tomatoes, about 2 pounds
1 tablespoon plus 1 teaspoon oil
salt
2 ounces shallots
8 parsley sprigs
grated rind of 2 lemons

1. Blanch **tomatoes** in boiling water for 1 minute, then plunge into cold water. Peel tomatoes, remove cores, and cut each one into halves from stem to blossom end. Press out as many seeds as possible. Preheat oven to 350°F.
2. Use 1 tablespoon **oil** to coat a casserole large enough to hold the tomato pieces in a single layer. Arrange the **tomato halves** in the casserole, and sprinkle each one with a tiny pinch of **salt.**
3. Peel **shallots,** and wash and dry **parsley.** Chop them together, then mince, and mix with **lemon rind.** Sprinkle the mixture over the tomatoes.
4. Brush the teaspoon of **oil** on a sheet of foil and press the oiled side down on the tomatoes. Braise the **tomatoes** for 20 minutes, or until as soft as you like them.
5. Remove the foil, and serve from the casserole. An excellent accompaniment to chicken or veal.

Tomatoes à la Diable

preparation time: 10 to 15 minutes
cooking time: 15 minutes, plus time to hard-cook eggs
serves 6

2 pounds firm ripe tomatoes
olive oil
3 hard-cooked egg yolks
2 ounces butter
2 teaspoons prepared Dijon mustard
3 tablespoons white-wine vinegar
2 uncooked eggs
chicken stock (optional)
1 teaspoon salt
1/8 teaspoon black pepper
dash of cayenne pepper

1. Blanch and peel **tomatoes,** and cut out cores. Cut tomatoes into thick slices and set on an oiled broiling pan.

2. Press **hard-cooked egg yolks** through a sieve. Melt **butter** in a small saucepan. Stir **mustard** into **vinegar.** Mix sieved egg yolks and mustard-vinegar into butter. Heat to a simmer. Remove from heat. Preheat broiler.

3. Beat **uncooked eggs** until well mixed but not frothy. Stir quickly into the **mustard-vinegar** mixture and return to heat. If mixture becomes too thick, add **stock,** 1 tablespoon at a time, to make a thick but not pasty mixture. Season sauce with **salt,** black **pepper,** and **cayenne.** Keep sauce warm over hot water.

4. Brush tomato slices lightly with **olive oil** and slide under preheated broiler. Broil for 3 minutes. Flip the slices over, brush second side with oil, and broil for 2 minutes longer.

5. Transfer **slices** to a shallow serving platter, and spoon **sauce** over them. Serve with roast beef or roast or grilled pork. Also good for vegetarian meals (this dish is protein-rich because of the eggs); serve with steamed or baked cracked wheat (bulgur) and green salad.

Curried Tomatoes, East Indian

preparation time: 15 minutes, plus time to prepare coconut
cooking time: 25 minutes
serves 8 to 10

3 pounds ripe tomatoes
2 yellow onions, about 8 ounces
1 garlic clove
1/2 ounce fresh gingerroot
3 tablespoons light sesame oil or mustard oil
1-1/2 teaspoons curry powder
1 cup chopped fresh coconut
chicken stock or vegetable broth
salt

1. Blanch and peel **tomatoes,** core them, and chop them. Peel and mince **onions.** Peel **garlic,** but leave it whole. Peel and mince **gingerroot.**
2. Heat **oil** in a large saucepan and sauté **garlic** until golden. Discard garlic. Add minced **onions** and **gingerroot** to the saucepan and sauté until onions are golden. Stir in **curry powder** and continue to sauté until the characteristic aroma of curry is released.
3. Add **tomatoes** and cook over low heat, stirring often, for 15 minutes. Stir in chopped **coconut** and cook for about 5 minutes longer. If the mixture becomes too dry, pour in **stock** or broth, a few tablespoons at a time.
4. Season with **salt** to taste. Serve with fish; or serve as a vegetarian dish with baked or steamed rice or millet.

variation: This tastes best with fresh ingredients. It can be made with canned plum tomatoes, ground ginger and flaked coconut without sweetening, but that is a second-best version. Save this recipe for times when you have fresh tomatoes, coconut and gingerroot. This is very pretty made with yellow tomatoes.

Curried Tomatoes, West Indian

preparation time: 10 minutes
cooking time: 10 to 15 minutes
serves 6

2 pounds ripe tomatoes
1/2 Bermuda onion
1 small hot pepper
2 tablespoons peanut oil
1 teaspoon curry powder
juice of 1 lime
salt

1. Blanch and peel **tomatoes,** core them, and chop them. Peel and mince **onion.** Wearing rubber or plastic gloves, remove stem, rib and seeds from **hot pepper** and chop it. Wash gloves before removing them.

2. Heat **oil** in a saucepan and add minced **onion.** Sauté over moderate heat until onion pieces are translucent. Stir in **curry powder** and continue to sauté until the characteristic aroma of curry is released.

3. Stir in **tomatoes** and **hot pepper** and simmer until tomatoes are somewhat reduced, almost to a lumpy purée.

4. Add **lime juice** and **salt** to taste. Serve with fish; also good with rice and other grain dishes.

variation: In winter, make this with drained canned peeled plum tomatoes. Use two 20-ounce cans.

23

Creole Tomatoes

preparation time: 10 to 15 minutes.
cooking time: 30 minutes
serves 6 to 8

2 pounds fresh tomatoes
1 onion, 4 ounces
1 large green bell pepper
1/2 pound fresh okra
2 tablespoons olive oil
1 teaspoon ground dried chiles
salt
1 tablespoon vinegar-packed capers

1. Blanch and peel **tomatoes,** core them, and chop them. Peel and mince **onion.** Wash **green pepper,** discard stem, ribs and seeds, and chop pepper. (If you wish, pepper can be roasted and peeled, or skin can be removed with a vegetable peeler.)
2. Drop whole **okra** pods into a pot of cold water, bring to a boil, and simmer for 3 minutes. Drain, rinse with cold water, and drain again. Cut off the little caps, and cut the pods into 1-inch crosswise slices.
3. Heat **oil** in a large saucepan and sauté **onion** and **green pepper** for 5 minutes, stirring often. Add **tomatoes** and cook for 10 minutes, stirring often. Mix in ground **chiles** and sliced **okra** and simmer for 10 minutes longer. Continue to stir, but gently, to avoid breaking up okra slices.
4. Add **salt** to taste and stir in the **capers.** Serve with beef steaks, fried chicken, plain white fish. Or spoon over white rice for vegetarian meals.

variation: Put the whole mixture into a 2-quart casserole and cover the top with soft fresh bread crumbs. Bake in a 350°F. oven until top is browned. Omit capers for this version and instead use 1/4 cup chopped pitted ripe olives.

Fried Green Tomatoes

preparation time: 10 minutes
cooking time: 20 minutes
serves 4 to 6

2 pounds green tomatoes
whole-wheat flour
1/4 cup olive oil, or more
salt and pepper
brown sugar

The green tomatoes rescued at the end of the season are usually small, and this recipe was made with small ones. If you have larger tomatoes, slice them accordingly and adjust the cooking time if necessary.

1. Wash and dry **tomatoes.** Cut a slice off at both stem and blossom end, and cut the rest of each tomato into 3 even slices.
2. Spoon out about 1/3 cup whole-wheat **flour** on a sheet of wax paper. Press each **tomato slice,** on both sides, onto the flour to make a light coating.
3. Heat 2 tablespoons of the **oil** in a large skillet and place as many floured slices in the pan as will fit in a single layer. Sauté them over moderate heat until golden on one side.
4. Turn slices over and sprinkle the browned side with a little **salt** and **pepper,** and a tiny pinch of **brown sugar** for each slice. Cook until second side is golden brown, again turn over, sprinkle again with seasoning and sugar, and then cover the pan for 2 minutes to be sure the slices are cooked in the middle.
5. Continue to sauté the **tomatoes,** adding more **oil** to the skillet for each batch. An excellent dish for breakfast, with sausage or ham, or a good accompaniment to chicken or ground turkey patties.

Tomato and Cheese Sandwiches

preparation time: 5 minutes
cooking time: about 5 minutes
serves 4

2 large tomatoes, about 1 pound
4 slices of firm bread (white, whole-wheat, oatmeal, cracked-wheat)
4 rather thick slices of Tilsit or Munster cheese
1 small onion, 1-1/2 ounces
3 to 4 tablespoons mayonnaise
1 teaspoon Italian seasoning
olive oil

1. Blanch and peel **tomatoes.** Cut 2 thick slices from the thickest part of each tomato. Use the rest of the fruit for another recipe. If you have smaller tomatoes, cut more slices, so that you have enough to make a layer on each sandwich.

2. Put **bread slices** on a baking sheet and toast under the broiler for about 2 minutes, until pale gold. Remove from broiler and turn slices upside down. The toasted side will be the bottom of the sandwich.

3. Arrange a slice of **cheese** on each piece of bread, then a **tomato slice.** Peel **onion** and cut into slivers. Divide slivers among tomatoes. Spread **mayonnaise** over tomatoes and sprinkle with **Italian seasoning.** Finally, use a feather pastry brush to flick a few drops of **olive oil** on top of each sandwich.

4. Slide the baking sheet under the broiler, and broil until the topping is brown and bubbly and the cheese melting.

Tomatoes Stuffed with Crab Meat Salad

preparation time: 15 minutes
cooking time: 1 minute for
blanching tomatoes
serves 4

4 ripe tomatoes, 8 to 10 ounces each
1 can (6-1/2 ounces) crab claws
1/4 cup minced fennel
1/2 cup minced celery
1/4 cup minced Spicy Sour Green Tomato Pickles (see Index)
1/4 cup mayonnaise
lemon juice or granulated fructose
salt and pepper
lettuce and fennel leaves

1. Blanch and peel **tomatoes.** Core them, and carefully scoop out the insides without damaging the shell. Put all the scooped-out portions in a strainer set over a bowl. Turn the hollowed tomatoes upside down to drain.
2. Put **crab claw meat** in a strainer, rinse with cold water, and remove any bits of shell or cartilage. Let crab meat drain well, then roll in paper towels to press out any remaining water. Put crab meat in a mixing bowl.
3. Prepare **fennel** and **celery,** using tender inner ribs in both cases. Part of the measured amount can be tender celery leaves and some of the feathery fennel leaves. Add minced **vegetables** and **pickles** to **crab,** then stir in **mayonnaise.** Chop enough of the scooped-out **tomato pulp** to have 1/4 cup, and mix that into the filling. (Use the drained juice and remaining pulp, with seeds removed, for sauce or soup.)
4. Taste and adjust with a little **lemon juice** if the salad is not acid enough or with a few pinches of **fructose** if it is too acid. Season with **salt** and **pepper** to taste.
5. Turn tomato shells upright, sprinkle very lightly with **salt,** and gently fill with **crab salad,** mounding it up in the center. Garnish each tomato with a sprig of **fennel** leaves, and place each one on a bed of shredded **lettuce** mixed with snipped **fennel** leaves. Serve for a luncheon or supper main course.

variations: If you cannot find canned crab claws in your market, use any other kind of crab meat, even fresh for special occasions. Add more mayonnaise if you wish. For another interesting taste accent, add a few drops of Pernod to the salad.

Baked Stuffed Tomatoes

preparation time: 15 minutes
cooking time: about 1 hour
serves 6

6 almost ripe tomatoes, about 8 ounces each
1 onion, 3 to 4 ounces
1/2 pound mushrooms
2 tablespoons olive oil
1-1/2 ounces butter
1 cup uncooked round-grain Italian rice
1 cup chicken stock, approximately
1 teaspoon salt
1/4 teaspoon ground turmeric
1/4 teaspoon ground cuminseed
juice of 1/2 lemon
6 parsley sprigs

Use tomatoes that are not completely ripe for this, as they will hold their shape better during baking. Also, when stuffing vegetables that are to be baked, it is best not to peel them, as the skin helps to hold the vegetable together.

1. Wash **tomatoes** carefully. Cut a slice straight across the top of each tomato. Carefully remove the core from these slices, but keep the slices, as they will serve as caps. Scoop out the pulp of the tomatoes, without damaging the shells, and put the pulp in a food mill set over a bowl. Set tomato shells upside down to drain.
2. Purée **tomato pulp** through the mill, leaving all the seeds in the mill. Measure the juice; there should be about 2 cups. Set aside.
3. Peel and mince the **onion.** Trim the **mushroom** stems and wipe mushrooms with a damp cloth. (Wash only if very dirty.) Chop mushrooms. Use some of the **oil** to coat a deep baking dish large enough to hold the tomatoes snugly. (Or each one can be baked in an individual baker.)
4. Heat remaining **oil** and the **butter** in a 2-quart saucepan. Sauté **onion** until translucent, then add **mushrooms** and continue to cook until they have released liquid and begin to brown. With a slotted spoon transfer both vegetables to a plate, leaving the oil in the saucepan. Don't worry if a few pieces of vegetable remain in the pan.

5. Put **rice** in the saucepan and sauté over low heat until kernels are opaque. Slowly pour in the reserved **tomato purée.** If there is less than 2 cups, add enough **chicken stock** to make up the difference. Stir in **salt, turmeric, cuminseed** and **lemon juice,** and bring to a boil. Cover, and simmer rice over low heat until the liquid is absorbed, about 12 minutes. Rice will be about two thirds cooked. Preheat oven to 350°F.

6. Remove **rice** from heat and gently stir in the sautéed **onion** and **mushrooms** and about 1/2 cup additional **chicken stock.** The mixture will be a little soupy. Spoon it into the drained tomato shells; do not press it in, but just fill; the rice will swell as it finishes cooking.

7. Set filled **tomatoes** in the oiled baking pan, and place each little cap on top. Bake for 20 to 30 minutes, until **rice** is completely tender. It will swell up and push the little caps awry, but no matter. Stick a **parsley sprig** in each cap where you cut out the core.

variation: For a more nutritious dish, add about 4 ounces of shredded cheese to the rice at the end of Step 5. An excellent main course for lunch or supper. For an Indian flavor, mix in 2 tablespoons dried currants and 2 tablespoons chopped blanched almonds or unroasted cashews.

Tomatoes Stuffed with Eggs

preparation time: 20 minutes
cooking time: 40 minutes
serves 6

6 firm tomatoes, about 8 ounces each
6 eggs
3 shallots
1 small zucchini, 4 ounces
1 tablespoon oil, plus oil for baking dish
2 ounces butter
3 tablespoons flour
1-1/2 cups chicken stock
salt and white pepper
1-1/2 ounces Parmesan cheese
3 flat anchovy fillets

1. Wash **tomatoes;** do not peel them. Cut a slice off the top of each one, and carefully scoop out the pulp without damaging the shells. Set shells upside down to drain. Chop the pulp and set it in a strainer to drain. Discard as many seeds as possible.

2. Cook the **eggs** in the shell to have "mollet" eggs, that is, for about 6 minutes. Immerse them at once in cold water. Shell them carefully, then gently lower them into a bowl of warm water to keep warm. If you find it easier to poach the eggs, do that. Trim the edges, and store in a bowl of warm water.

3. Peel and mince **shallots.** Scrape **zucchini** and shred it in a food processor fitted with the shredding disk.

4. Heat 1 tablespoon **oil** and 1 tablespoon **butter.** Add **shallots** and sauté until translucent. Add **zucchini** and sauté for 1 minute. Mix in 3/4 cup of the drained chopped **tomato pulp** and cook over low heat until you have a thick mixture. Set aside.

5. Melt remaining **butter** in a separate pan. Stir in the **flour,** then pour in **chicken stock** and cook over low heat, stirring often, until sauce is thickened. Set aside.

6. Turn **tomatoes** right side up. Use the rest of the **oil** to coat a baking dish or individual bakers. Spoon about 1 tablespoon of the **vegetable mixture** in the bottom of each tomato. Gently drop 1 **egg,** well drained and dried, into each tomato. Spoon another tablespoon of the vegetables over each egg. Grate the **cheese.** Preheat oven to 400°F.

7. Turn remaining **vegetables** into the **sauce** and purée the mixture in the food processor fitted with the steel blade. Return to the saucepan and heat. Stir in 1 ounce of the grated **cheese.** Season the sauce with more **salt** to taste (you won't need much since cheese is salty) and a little **pepper.**

8. Place **tomatoes** in the baking dish, and spoon about 1/4 cup **sauce** over each tomato. Sprinkle remaining **cheese** on top. Bake in the preheated oven for 10 to 15 minutes, until tomatoes are soft and very hot and the cheese topping golden. Split the **anchovy fillets** and arrange 1 thin strip in a twist on top of each tomato. Serve for a brunch, luncheon main course, or supper dish.

variation: This dish is perhaps a little fussy and complicated, although no step is difficult. A number of simpler versions will occur to you. Beaten raw eggs mixed with vegetables and cheese can be baked in tomato shells for a sort of vegetable custard. Hard-cooked eggs, chopped, in cheese sauce offer another possibility for stuffing.

31

Tomatoes Filled with Cheese Soufflé

preparation time: 15 minutes
cooking time: about 40
minutes
serves 6

6 large tomatoes, each 7 to 8 ounces
3 small shallots
1 ounce unsalted butter
2 tablespoons all-purpose flour
1/2 cup milk
1/2 cup chicken stock
2 ounces blue cheese
2 ounces cream cheese
3 egg yolks
5 egg whites
salt
oil

1. Wash **tomatoes;** do not peel them. Cut a small slice off the top of each one, and carefully scoop out the pulp without damaging the shells. Set shells upside down to drain. The scooped-out pulp is not used in the recipe; save it for sauce or soup.

2. Peel and mince **shallots.** Melt **butter** in a saucepan and sauté shallots until tender and golden. Stir in the **flour,** then slowly add **milk** and **stock** to make a thick sauce. Remove from heat.

3. Crumble both **cheeses** and stir into the sauce. The cheese will melt in the retained heat of the sauce.

4. Beat **egg yolks.** Mix in a little of the **sauce** to warm yolks, then turn into the rest of the sauce. Let the sauce cool. Heat oven to 375°F.

5. Beat **egg whites** and a pinch of **salt** with a rotary egg beater until stiff peaks stand up straight when beater is withdrawn. Use a rubber spatula to fold about a third of egg whites into the cheese sauce, then very gently fold in the rest.

6. Oil a large baking dish. Set **tomato shells** in the dish. Gently spoon **soufflé batter** into the tomatoes, making them about three quarters full. Bake them for about 25 minutes, until soufflés are well puffed up and tomatoes soft. Serve as a first course, with toast and watercress.

variations: Use Cheddar cheese instead of the blue and cream cheeses; or use a mixture of Gruyère and Parmesan. For a richer dish, use 1 cup light cream in place of milk and stock. The soufflé batter may rise over the tops of the tomatoes and spill over. Scoop up the spilled soufflé and serve it. Or tomatoes may split; that spoils the appearance but not the taste. If there is extra batter, bake it in custard cups or a small casserole.

Tomato Pilaf

preparation time: 15 minutes
cooking time: 20 minutes
serves 6

1 pound ripe plum tomatoes
4 shallots
2 tablespoons vegetable oil or light sesame oil
1 cup uncooked long-grain rice
1-1/2 cups chicken stock or mushroom broth or water
1 teaspoon salt
1 tablespoon lemon juice
6 parsley sprigs
rind of 2 lemons

1. Blanch and peel **tomatoes.** Cut out cores, and cut tomatoes from stem to blossom end into halves. Scoop out the center part of tomatoes into a food mill, and purée to remove the seeds. Measure the purée. Chop the rest of the tomatoes into small cubes, about the size of a large green pea. Set **purée** and **cubes** aside in separate containers.
2. Peel and mince **shallots.** Heat **oil** in a 2-quart saucepan and sauté shallots until translucent. Add **rice** and stir it in the oil until kernels are opaque.
3. Meanwhile combine **tomato purée** with enough of the **stock,** broth or water to make 2 cups liquid. Pour it slowly into the rice, stirring all the while. Add **salt** and **lemon juice** and bring to a boil. Cover and simmer for 10 minutes.
4. Uncover the saucepan and gently stir in the **tomato cubes.** Cover the pan and cook for about 8 minutes longer, or until rice is cooked to your taste.
5. While rice is cooking, chop **lemon rind** and **parsley** in a food processor fitted with the steel blade. (Or grate the rind and mince the parsley.) Turn **rice** into a deep serving bowl and sprinkle parsley mixture around the edge. Or, if you prefer, stir the parsley mixture into the rice before serving. Excellent with veal, chicken and fish.

Tomato Pudding

preparation time: 15 minutes
cooking time: 1 hour
serves 6 to 8

2 pounds tomatoes
1 tablespoon sugar
2 teaspoons salt
1/2 pound sliced oatmeal or cracked-wheat bread
4 to 6 ounces Cheddar cheese
butter for casserole

1. Blanch and peel **tomatoes.** Cut out cores, and chop tomatoes, making about 1-inch cubes. Mix in the **sugar** and **salt.**
2. Cut crusts from **bread** and cut slices into 1/2-inch cubes. Shred the **cheese. Butter** a 2-quart casserole. Preheat oven to 375°F.
3. Mix **tomatoes, bread cubes** and **cheese** together and spoon into the casserole. Cover with a buttered sheet of foil. Bake for about 1 hour. Toward the end, remove the foil to let the top brown a little.

variations: In winter, when fresh tomatoes are lacking, make this with canned peeled plum tomatoes. Use two 20-ounce cans, and drain off most of the juice for other uses (it makes the pudding too wet). Chop the canned tomatoes coarsely.
If you change the cheese, you change the flavor. Other good cheeses in this pudding are Jarlsberg, Gouda, whole-milk mozzarella. If you like, some grated Parmesan or Romano can be sprinkled on top for a golden-brown finish.

Tomato Torta

preparation time: 15 minutes
cooking time: 40 minutes
serves 6

2 pounds fresh tomatoes
1 leek or 1 onion
1 small zucchini, about 4 ounces
8 medium-size mushrooms
1 Italian green pepper
3 tablespoons olive oil
4 eggs
salt and pepper
1 ounce Parmesan or Romano cheese
chopped parsley

1. Blanch and peel **tomatoes,** core them, and chop them. Wash **leek,** cut into crosswise slices, and wash again; or peel and chop **onion.** Scrape **zucchini,** and grate; or cut into small cubes. Trim **mushroom** stems and wipe mushrooms with a damp cloth. Chop mushrooms. Wash **green pepper,** discard stem, ribs and seeds, and cut into small squares.
2. Use a little of the **oil** to coat a deep 9-inch glass pie dish or 6-cup porcelain quiche dish.
3. Heat remaining **oil** in large skillet and sauté **leek** or **onion** until translucent. Add **mushrooms** and **green pepper** and sauté until almost tender. Finally add **zucchini** and sauté for another 2 minutes. Set aside.
4. Cook **tomatoes** over low heat, stirring often, until they are reduced almost to a purée. Stir **tomatoes** into the **sautéed vegetables.** (If you prefer, tomatoes can be puréed through a food mill to remove seeds.) Preheat oven to 350°F.
5. Beat **eggs** in a large bowl until well mixed but not frothy. Add all the **vegetables,** mix well, and season with **salt** and freshly ground black **pepper** to taste.
6. Pour the mixture into the oiled dish. Cover with a sheet of foil, and bake in the oven for about 20 minutes, until the eggs are firm.
7. While torta is baking, grate the **cheese.** As soon as the dish is finished, sprinkle top with cheese. Cut into pie-shaped pieces, and garnish with chopped **parsley.** Serve for a luncheon or supper main dish.

Tomato Soufflé

preparation time: 15 minutes
cooking time: about 50
minutes, plus time to
prepare tomato purée
serves 6

1-1/2 ounces butter
1/2 ounce Parmesan or Romano cheese
3 white onions (silverskins)
1/2 teaspoon curry powder
2 tablespoons flour
1/2 cup light cream
1/2 cup chicken stock or tomato juice
1 cup Thick Tomato Purée (see Index)
2 ounces white Cheddar or Jarlsberg cheese
salt
4 egg yolks
5 egg whites

1. Use 1 tablespoon of the **butter** to coat the inside of a 6-cup soufflé dish. Grate **Parmesan cheese** and sprinkle it over the butter coating to cover dish completely.

2. Peel and mince **onions.** Melt remaining **butter** in a saucepan and sauté onions until translucent. Sprinkle in **curry powder,** cook for 1 minute, then off the heat stir in **flour.** Pour in **cream** and **stock** and simmer, stirring, until sauce is very thick. Gently stir in **tomato purée** and remove pan from heat.

3. Grate **Cheddar** or **Jarlsberg cheese** and stir it into the thick sauce; it will melt in the retained heat of the sauce. Stir now and then to mix. Taste, and add **salt** if needed.

4. Beat **egg yolks,** then mix in 1/2 cup of the hot **sauce** and blend well. Return to the rest of the sauce, mix, and let the sauce cool. Preheat oven to 375°F.

5. Beat **egg whites** with a pinch of **salt** until stiff but not dry. Fold one third of whites into the cooled sauce, then gently fold in the remainder; do not overfold.

6. Spoon the **batter** into the prepared dish. With a knife blade, indent a ring around the top 1 inch in from the edge. Bake soufflé for about 40 minutes, until well puffed-up and beginning to brown. Serve at once.

Spanish Rice

preparation time: 15 minutes
cooking time: 30 to 40 minutes
serves 6

1 cup long-grain rice or brown rice
1/2 cup blanched almonds
3 tablespoons olive oil
1 Spanish onion, about 4 ounces
1 green pepper, about 6 ounces
1 pound ripe tomatoes
1 cup chicken stock or water
1 teaspoon salt
juice of 1 lemon
1/2 teaspoon crumbled dried orégano
1/2 cup chopped pitted black olives or green ripe olives

1. Wash **rice** in several changes of water; drain well, and roll in a cloth towel to dry. Or skip this step entirely if you prefer.

2. Chop **almonds.** Heat 1 tablespoon **oil** in a large saucepan and sauté almonds until golden. Lift them out and drain them on paper towels.

3. Peel and mince **onion.** Wash **green pepper;** discard stem, ribs and seeds, and mince pepper. Wash **tomatoes,** core them, and chop. (If you prefer, pepper can be skinned by roasting and tomatoes can be peeled by blanching, but the Mexicans who make this don't usually bother to do either.)

4. Add remaining **oil** to saucepan and sauté **onion** and **pepper** until onion is translucent. Stir in **rice** until well coated with oil. Add chopped **tomatoes, stock** or water, **salt, lemon juice** and **orégano.** Stir to mix everything well.

5. Bring to a boil, reduce to a simmer, cover the saucepan, and cook for 20 minutes, or until all the liquid is absorbed and rice is very tender. Stir in the sautéed **almonds** and the **olives.**

variations: At the end of Step 4, turn the mixture into an oiled 6-cup casserole and bake it in a 350°F. oven for 40 minutes, or until rice is very tender.

To make a hotter dish, use 2 fresh green chiles instead of the green pepper. Use rubber or plastic gloves to split them, and discard stems, ribs and seeds. Chop into small pieces.

Tomato Quiche

preparation time: 30 minutes
cooking time: 45 to 50 minutes, plus time to prepare tomato purée
serves 12 as an appetizer or snack, 4 to 6 as a luncheon or supper main dish

1 pound short pastry
2-1/2 ounces butter
8 medium-size plum tomatoes, about 1 pound
2 large leeks
salt
3 eggs
1/2 cup light cream
2 tablespoons minced fresh parsley
1 cup Thick Tomato Purée (see Index)
white pepper
lemon juice (optional)

1. Make the **pastry** (or use frozen or packaged pastry), and roll it out to a sheet about 1/8 inch thick. Butter a 10-inch porcelain quiche dish and gently fit pastry, without stretching it, into the dish. Press to the sides and trim off excess pastry. Set aside in a cool place.

2. Blanch and peel **tomatoes,** halve them, and press out as many seeds as possible. Melt 1 ounce of the **butter** in a heavy skillet and arrange the tomato halves in a single layer. Cover with a sheet of foil with a small hole in the center. Over low heat braise **tomatoes** until they are soft and tender but still hold their shape.

3. Meanwhile, wash **leeks** carefully, slice them across including 2 inches of the green part, and wash again. Heat another ounce of the **butter** and gently cook drained leeks until very tender. Preheat oven to 375°F.

4. Beat **eggs** and **cream** in a bowl. Stir in **parsley** and thick **tomato purée** and season with **salt** and **white pepper** to taste. Add a few drops of **lemon juice** if you like. Spoon the mixture into the pastry. Arrange the braised **tomato halves** around the edge, alternating with a spoonful of the braised **leeks.** Any remaining braised vegetables can be fitted in the center, making a pattern. Cover loosely with a sheet of foil.

5. Bake in the oven for 15 minutes, then remove the foil and continue baking for 15 minutes longer. Serve hot, cold, or at room temperature.

variations: For a more nutritious quiche, add 4 ounces prosciutto, chopped, or 4 ounces smoked haddock, rinsed in boiling water and cut into 1-inch pieces. This will give you extra filling and you may need a 12-inch dish; or make 2 quiches.

Skewered Swordfish and Cherry Tomatoes

preparation time: 20 minutes,
plus 1 hour for marinating
cooking time: 10 minutes
serves 6

2 pounds swordfish steak
1 garlic clove
1 ounce fresh gingerroot
juice of 4 limes
1/4 cup olive oil
1/2 teaspoon ground coriander
2 Bermuda onions, 6 to 7 ounces each
18 cherry tomatoes
18 small mushrooms

1. Trim **swordfish** of all fatty edges, skin and bones. Cut steak into pieces about 1-1/2 inches square and as thick as the steak. There should be at least 24 pieces. Place swordfish in a glass or pottery container.
2. Peel **garlic** and **gingerroot** and drop into the bowl of a food processor fitted with a steel blade. Add **lime juice, oil** and **coriander,** and process until emulsified. Pour over the **swordfish,** turn to coat all the pieces, and let them marinate for 1 hour.
3. Peel **onions,** cut into 4 quarters, and cut each quarter into 3 pieces. Wash **tomatoes** and remove stems. Remove **mushroom** stems (save for soup or sauce) and wipe caps with a damp cloth.
4. Use 6 steel skewers. Thread 4 pieces of **swordfish,** 3 pieces of **onion,** 3 whole **tomatoes** and 3 **mushroom caps** on each skewer, beginning and ending with swordfish. Brush any remaining **marinade** over the ingredients.
5. Broil skewers in an indoor broiler 5 inches from the source of heat for about 3 minutes on each side, or until fish is done to your taste. Or grill them on an outdoor barbecue; outside, brush skewers with remaining marinade, or lacking that use a little extra oil, to prevent drying. Turn the skewers to brown on all sides.

Sole Dugléré

preparation time: 15 minutes
cooking time: 25 minutes
serves 6

6 fillets of lemon sole, about 6 ounces each
4 shallots
1 garlic clove
1-1/2 pounds tomatoes
2-1/2 ounces butter
1/4 cup chopped fresh parsley
salt and white pepper
6 ounces dry white wine
1/2 cup tomato juice
2 teaspoons flour
6 tiny parsley or watercress sprigs

Tomatoes are the chief ingredient of the Dugléré garnish. This dish is named for Adolphe Dugléré, chef at the Café Anglais in Paris, who invented it during the latter part of the last century. This is a simplified version of his preparation.

1. Rinse **sole fillets** and pat dry. Peel and mince **shallots.** Peel **garlic** and put through a press.
2. Blanch and peel **tomatoes,** core them, and cut them into halves. Gently press out all the seeds. Chop tomatoes.
3. Melt 1 ounce of the **butter** in a skillet and sauté **shallots** and **garlic** until golden. Add **tomatoes** and cook gently, stirring often, until tomatoes are almost puréed. Preheat oven to 350°F.
4. Use another ounce of the **butter** to coat a flameproof baking dish about 10 × 7 inches. Spoon half of the **tomato mixture** on the bottom and sprinkle with half of the **parsley.**
5. Sprinkle **sole fillets** with **salt** and **white pepper,** and roll them up. Arrange them in a single layer on the vegetable bed. Cover with remaining **vegetables** and sprinkle with remaining **parsley.** Gently pour **wine** and **tomato juice** into the pan; liquid should reach about halfway to the top of the rolls. Cover the fish with a sheet of foil or wax paper, and make a small hole in it for the steam to escape.
6. Set the baking dish over moderate heat and bring liquid to a boil. Cover the dish and transfer it to the oven. Oven-poach **fillets** for 10 minutes; they should be tender, but not dried. Gently transfer the rolls to a serving platter, cover loosely with a sheet of foil, and keep them warm.

7. Pour all the **cooking juices** and **vegetables** into the container of a blender, or into the bowl of a food processor fitted with the steel blade. Process until puréed.

8. Spoon or pour **purée** into a skillet and cook over low heat, stirring often, until reduced to about 1-1/2 cups. Mix remaining **butter** with **flour** to make beurre manié, and crumble it into the simmering sauce to thicken it. Stir to blend and add **salt** and **pepper** if needed.

9. Spoon **sauce** over the **sole fillets.** Garnish each one with a **parsley** or **watercress sprig.**

variations: If you can find Dover sole, fresh or frozen, use that; the fillets will be somewhat larger and thicker, so you may find it easier to split them for rolling.

The sauce can be enriched with a liaison of 1 egg yolk and 1/2 cup heavy cream, if you wish. More elaborate garnishes, of puff-pastry crescents, tiny rice molds, cherry tomatoes or sculptured mushrooms, can be added.

Flounder with Tomato and Cheese

preparation time: 15 minutes
cooking time: 10 minutes
serves 4

4 flounder fillets, 5 ounces each
1 tomato, about 6 ounces
1 white onion, 2 ounces
2 tablespoons olive oil
4 tablespoons chopped parsley
4 slices of cheese (Havarti, Gouda, mild Cheddar)

1. Rinse **flounder fillets** and pat dry. Blanch and peel **tomato.** Cut 4 thick slices from the middle (use the rest of the tomato for another recipe). Peel and mince **onion.** Preheat broiler.

2. Heat **oil** in a large skillet and sauté **onion** until golden. Add half of the **parsley.** After a few seconds, put in the **flounder fillets,** in a single layer, and sauté for 1-1/2 minutes on each side. Transfer fillets to a baking sheet. (No need to oil the baking sheet.)

3. Sprinkle **onion** and **parsley** from the skillet over the fish. Place 1 slice of **tomato** on each fillet, and a slice of **cheese** on top of each tomato. Slide under the broiler and broil until cheese is melted.

4. Sprinkle with the rest of the **parsley** and serve at once.

41

Basque Fish

preparation time: 15 minutes
cooking time: about 45
    minutes
serves 6

6 pieces of cod, haddock or hake, either steaks or fillets, 2 to 3 pounds
2 Spanish onions, about 4 ounces each
2 pounds fresh tomatoes
6 garlic cloves, unpeeled
3 large red bell peppers
1/2 cup olive oil
salt and pepper
3 tablespoons vinegar-packed capers, drained
lemon juice
24 oil-cured black olives, pitted

1. Rinse **fish pieces** and pat dry. Peel **onions** and cut from top to bottom into thick shreds. Blanch and peel **tomatoes,** and chop them.

2. Put unpeeled **garlic cloves** in a small pan of water and simmer until garlic is tender. Roast the **peppers** until skin is charred, then peel them and discard stems, ribs and seeds. Or if you prefer, peel peppers with a swivel vegetable peeler. Cut peppers into slivers.

3. Heat 3 tablespoons of the **oil** in a skillet and cook the **tomatoes** until they are reduced to a purée. Squeeze the **garlic cloves** to press out the pulp and add it to the tomatoes. Put the whole mixture through a food mill.

4. Heat another 3 tablespoons of the **oil** in the skillet and sauté **onion shreds** and **pepper slivers** until tender. Transfer to a plate. Preheat oven to 350°F.

5. Add remaining **oil** to skillet and gently sauté the **fish pieces,** a few at a time, until just golden. Sprinkle them with **salt** and **pepper.** Spoon a little of the **tomato** and **garlic purée** into a shallow baking dish and arrange the **fish** on top. If they are steaks, place in a single layer; if they are fillets, they may need to be folded or overlapped.

6. Stir **capers** into remaining purée, then gently fold in sautéed **onions** and **peppers.** Taste, and add a little **salt** and **pepper** if needed, also a little **lemon juice** to taste. Spoon the mixture over the fish and cover with an oiled sheet of foil.

7. Bake the **fish** in the oven for about 15 minutes, or until sauce is bubbly and fish done to your taste. Sprinkle with the **olives.** Serve from the baking dish. Accompany with steamed or boiled new potatoes sprinkled with parsley, and a green salad with oranges and lime dressing.

Chicken Hunter Style (Pollo alla Cacciatora)

preparation time: 25 minutes
cooking time: about 40 minutes
serves 4

1 frying chicken, about 3 pounds
1 onion, 2 ounces
1 garlic clove
1 green pepper, about 6 ounces
1-1/2 pounds plum tomatoes
1/4 cup olive oil
1/4 cup chopped parsley
2 fresh basil leaves, or 1/2 teaspoon dried basil
salt and pepper
4 ounces dry white wine
1/2 pound fresh mushrooms

1. Cut **chicken** into serving pieces—wings, legs, second joints, and cut each breast portion into 2 fillets. Save wing tips, neck and bony back portion for stock, and save liver for a breakfast omelet. Gizzard and heart can be used in this dish. Rinse pieces and pat dry.

2. Peel and chop **onion.** Peel **garlic** and put through a press. Wash and trim **pepper;** discard stem, ribs and seeds; cut pepper into lengthwise slivers. Wash and core **tomatoes,** and chop them.

3. Heat 2 tablespoons **oil** in a large deep skillet, and brown the **chicken** pieces, a few at a time. As the pieces are browned, transfer to a plate. When all are done, pour off the fat and wipe out the skillet.

4. Pour remaining **oil** into the same skillet and sauté **onion** and **garlic** until golden. Add **pepper slivers** and cook only until lightly browned. Add **tomatoes, parsley** and **basil,** and cook until tomatoes are soft and somewhat reduced.

5. Sprinkle **chicken pieces** with **salt** and **pepper** and return them to the skillet. Spoon some of the vegetable mixture over the pieces. Pour in the **wine,** cover the skillet, and simmer for about 20 minutes, or until chicken is done to your taste.

6. While chicken cooks, trim **mushroom** stems, wipe mushrooms with a damp cloth, and slice them. About 5 minutes before chicken is done, add **mushrooms** to skillet and stir to mix with **vegetables.**

7. Serve with risotto made with round-grain Italian rice and a green salad.

variations: Omit garlic, or sauté the whole clove briefly before putting onion in the pan. For a more refined dish, roast the pepper and remove the skin, and blanch and peel tomatoes. Use red wine instead of white. At the end, add a dozen pitted black olives.

Italian Beef Stew

preparation time: 15 minutes
cooking time: about 2-1/2 hours
serves 4

1-1/2 pounds boneless lean beef
1-1/2 pounds ripe plum tomatoes
2 celery ribs
2 tablespoons olive oil
1/2 cup chopped fresh parsley
2 fresh basil leaves, or 1/2 teaspoon dried
1/4 teaspoon crumbled dried orégano
1/4 teaspoon crumbled dried thyme
salt and pepper
3 ounces butter
1/2 cup dry white wine
1 sprig of rosemary, or 1 teaspoon dried
1 large garlic clove
8 thick slices of Italian bread

Use cross-rib or top sirloin (from the round) for best flavor and texture in this stew.

1. Cut **beef** into 1-1/2-inch cubes. Wash and core **tomatoes** and chop them. Wash and dry **celery,** and chop to make about 3/4 cup.
2. Heat **oil** in a heavy saucepan and add **tomatoes, celery, parsley, basil** and **dried herbs.** Cover, bring to a boil, then simmer for about 30 minutes, until reduced to sauce consistency. Put through a food mill and set aside. Season with **salt** and **pepper** to taste.
3. Melt 2 ounces of the **butter** in a 2-quart top-of-stove casserole and brown the **beef cubes;** they should lose all the red color. Lift cubes out to a plate.
4. Pour the **wine** into the casserole and over low heat reduce it to 1/4 cup. Return **beef cubes,** pour in **tomato sauce,** and add the **rosemary.** Cover the casserole and simmer for 1-1/2 to 2 hours.
5. Peel and split **garlic** and rub over the slices of **bread.** Brush remaining ounce of **butter** on the slices. Toast them, buttered side up, in the broiler or in a toaster-oven.
6. Place 2 slices of **toast** in each of 4 hot deep soup plates, and ladle **beef** and **sauce** over them.

variation: When fresh tomatoes are lacking, use 3 cups canned peeled plum tomatoes packed with basil and omit the basil in the ingredients.

Tomato Salad

preparation time: 10 minutes,
plus 1 hour for marinating
serves 6

1-1/2 pounds fully ripe tomatoes
3 tablespoons minced fresh parsley
3 tablespoons snipped fresh chives
salt and pepper
1 tablespoon olive oil
1 tablespoon lemon juice
1 bunch of watercress (optional)

Make this only when you have perfect tomatoes, preferably picked after ripening completely. Greenhouse or hydroponic fruits do not have enough flavor for this salad.

1. Blanch and peel **tomatoes.** Remove cores and cut into rather thick slices, either crosswise or from stem to blossom end; or cut into thin wedges if you prefer. Arrange slices, slightly overlapping, on a round salad platter, or on individual plates.
2. Mix **parsley** and **chives** and sprinkle evenly over **tomatoes.** Do not season yet. Cover the platter or plates with a sheet of wax paper or clear plastic wrap and let them rest at room temperature for about 1 hour.
3. At serving time, season **tomatoes** with **salt** and grind **black pepper** to taste over them. Mix **olive oil** and **lemon juice;** with a feather brush flick the dressing in tiny droplets over all the tomatoes.
4. If you wish, **watercress** can be used as a garnish. Cut off the bottom of the stems, wash cress carefully, and roll in a towel to dry. Use the leafy tips only; save stems for soup. Just before serving arrange the sprigs around the platter or plates. Do not do this earlier, or cress will become limp.

variation: Follow the Provençal taste, and mix 1 garlic clove, put through a press, with the parsley and chives before sprinkling the mixture on the tomatoes.

Tomato Salad with Yogurt Dressing

preparation time: 10 to 15 minutes, plus 1 hour for marinating
cooking time: 10 minutes
serves 6

2 green peppers, 6 ounces each
1 large cucumber
salt and pepper
1/4 cup olive oil
2 tablespoons fresh lemon juice
1 cup plain yogurt
2 large ripe tomatoes, 8 to 10 ounces each
snipped fresh dill

1. Blanch **green peppers** in boiling water for 10 minutes; drain, rinse with cold water, and drain again. (If you prefer, peppers can be charred and peeled instead of blanched.) Discard stems, ribs and seeds, and chop peppers.
2. Peel **cucumber,** halve lengthwise, and scoop out seeds. Chop cucumber and mix with **peppers** in a pottery or glass bowl. Sprinkle with **salt** and **pepper,** mix well, then pour in **olive oil** and **lemon juice.** Mix again, then cover and marinate for about 1 hour.
3. Pour off and reserve the **marinade.** Spoon **yogurt** into the **vegetables** and gently mix. Add some of the marinade to adjust the texture; it should be thick but not stiff.
4. Blanch and peel **tomatoes,** core them, and cut each into 3 thick slices. (The end pieces can be used for something else.)
5. Place 1 **tomato slice** on each of 6 salad plates and spoon part of the **yogurt mixture** on each one. Sprinkle snipped **dill** on top.

46

Tomatoes with Pesto and Anchovies

preparation time: 15 to 20
minutes
serves 6

2 cups packed fresh basil leaves
3 ounces pecorino Romano cheese
4 garlic cloves
1 ounce pine nuts, about 2 tablespoons
1/3 cup olive oil
2 pounds ripe tomatoes, about 6
12 flat anchovy fillets

Pesto, from Genoa, and pistou, from Provence, are similar; both are made from basil, garlic and oil. Only a little of this pungent sauce gives a special savor to soups and sauces. The flavors are especially delicious with ripe tomatoes.

1. First make the pesto. Wash **basil leaves** and roll in a towel to dry. Grate the **cheese** in a food processor fitted with the steel blade. Pour out the cheese onto a plate. Peel **garlic** and drop into the processor with the **basil leaves** and **pine nuts.** Mince, then add the **cheese** and mix. With the motor running, pour the **oil,** 1 tablespoon at a time, through the tube until the mixture is thick. Any pesto not used in the recipe can be refrigerated or frozen.
2. Blanch and peel **tomatoes.** Cut them into thick slices. Use a flexible spreader to coat each slice with a thin layer of pesto. Arrange the slices on 6 salad plates.
3. Blot excess oil from **anchovies** with a paper towel and arrange 2 fillets on each plate. Serve as a first course.

variations: Arrange 1 anchovy fillet on each tomato slice and serve them as one of hors-d'oeuvre variés.
Instead of anchovies, use 2 or 3 poached fresh shrimps for each serving. Split them, and arrange a half on each tomato slice.
Rugola, watercress or endive can be added to the salads to make them more substantial.
If you do not have a processor, pesto can be made in the traditional way: crush the solids in a large mortar and keep mashing as you add the oil. When pine nuts are too expensive, walnuts are a fine substitute.

47

Tricolor Salad

preparation time: 15 minutes
serves 6

2 small avocados
1 large lemon
2 large ripe red tomatoes
2 large ripe yellow tomatoes
3 cups shredded lettuce
3 tablespoons olive oil
salt and pepper
3 tablespoons minced parsley, or mixed fresh coriander and parsley

Make this when you have both red and yellow tomatoes. Add more dressing if you like.

1. Peel **avocados,** halve them, discard pits, and cut each half into 1/2-inch slices. Squeeze the **lemon.** Use a pastry brush or a lettuce leaf to brush all the avocado slices with lemon juice. Blanch all the **tomatoes** and cut them into thin wedges.
2. Divide the **lettuce** among 6 salad plates, or arrange on a round serving platter. Arrange the slices of **avocado** and **red** and **yellow tomato wedges** alternately on the lettuce.
3. Mix remaining **lemon juice,** the **olive oil** and **seasoning** to taste. Whisk well, then sprinkle dressing over the salads. Finally scatter **minced herbs** on top.
4. This salad can be multiplied as needed; it makes a beautiful salad for a buffet meal.

Tomato Salad with Walnuts

preparation time: 15 minutes
serves 6

1 bunch of watercress
3 large very ripe tomatoes, about 1-1/2 pounds
4 ounces shelled walnuts
3/4 cup dairy sour cream
1 teaspoon salt
dash of black pepper
juice of 1 lime
1/2 cup snipped fresh chives

1. Trim **watercress** stems, wash cress, drain, and roll in a towel to dry. Divide cress among 6 salad plates.
2. Blanch and peel **tomatoes.** Cut them into thick slices or wedges and divide among the salad plates.
3. Chop **walnuts** and sprinkle over tomatoes. Measure **sour cream** into a bowl and beat with a whisk to lighten. Season it with **salt** and **pepper** and mix in the **lime juice.**
4. Spoon equal amounts of **sour cream** over the salads and sprinkle **chives** on top. Serve as a salad or as a first course.

Tomato Aspic

preparation time: 10 minutes
plus 2 hours for chilling
cooking time: 30 minutes
serves 6 to 8

2 pounds fully ripe tomatoes
1/2 Bermuda onion, 4 to 6 ounces
2 large celery ribs with leaves
1 teaspoon salt
1 large bay leaf
2 whole cloves
2 teaspoons sugar or bland honey
2 to 3 envelopes (7 grams each) unflavored gelatin
1/2 to 3/4 cup cold water
2 to 3 teaspoons fresh lemon juice

This is a simple basic aspic. It can be modified by using other herbs and spices; it can be molded in individual or large containers, in shaped molds or tiny molds, or filled into hollowed-out vegetables. Or it can be poured into a sheet pan, to be cut into large cubes or diamonds, or into small diamonds for garnish.

1. Wash the **tomatoes,** cut them into small pieces, and put in a large heavy kettle. Peel and chop **onion** and add to tomatoes. Wash **celery,** cut into pieces, and add to tomatoes. Add **salt, bay leaf, cloves** and **sugar.**
2. Bring mixture to a boil, then simmer for 20 to 30 minutes.
3. Discard **bay leaf** and **cloves.** Put the whole mixture through a food mill or force through a sieve. Measure the purée.
4. For each 1-3/4 cups **purée,** use 1 envelope **gelatin** and 1/4 cup **cold water** flavored with 1 teaspoon **lemon juice.** Put the water and lemon juice in a small saucepan and sprinkle gelatin over it.
5. When gelatin is softened, pour in 1 cup of the hot **tomato purée,** set the saucepan over low heat, and stir until gelatin is completely dissolved. Pour into the rest of the purée, stir, set aside to cool.
6. When mixture is cool, pour it into a 4- to 6-cup round or star-shaped or ring mold that has been rinsed in cold water; or use 6 to 8 individual 6-ounce molds or custard cups. Set mold or cups on a baking sheet and slide into refrigerator; be sure the sheet is level. Chill for 2 hours, or until firm.
7. To unmold, place a wet plate upside down on the mold and turn plate and mold upside down. Loosen the jelly with the blade of a knife, and gently shake it out onto the plate. (The moisture on the plate makes it possible to move the aspic to center it.)
8. Surround with salad greens and garnish with parsley or watercress.

Tomato Salad Dressing

preparation time: 10 minutes
cooking time: 10 minutes
makes about 2 cups

1 pound very ripe tomatoes
salt
1 whole clove
2 teaspoons dry mustard
1/4 cup cider vinegar
2 drops of Tabasco
1 cup olive oil
sugar (optional)
1 garlic clove

1. Wash **tomatoes,** chop, and put in a heavy saucepan with 1/2 teaspoon **salt.** Crush the **clove** in a mortar and add to the tomatoes. Bring to a simmer, stirring often to prevent burning. Simmer for 10 minutes.

2. Put **tomatoes** through a food mill, then through a sieve, to make a thin purée. Measure 1 cup purée. The rest can be refrigerated for another use.

3. Mix the dressing shortly before you plan to use it. Stir **mustard** into **vinegar** until dissolved. Add **Tabasco.** With a whisk combine **vinegar, oil** and **tomato purée.** Adjust the **salt** to your taste. You may want to add a little sugar if the tomatoes are very acid.

4. Peel **garlic** and thread on a string or wooden food pick and drop into the dressing. Remove garlic before serving. Shake well or whisk again before serving. Use for salads of mixed greens, vegetables, or fish. Makes about 2 cups.

variations: In seasons when very ripe tomatoes are not available, use 2 cups canned peeled plum tomatoes, or even canned tomato purée. In a pinch tomato juice will do, although it makes a thin-textured dressing.

51

Thick Tomato Purée (Coulis de Tomates)

preparation time: 20 minutes
cooking time: 30 minutes
makes about 3 cups

3 pounds ripe tomatoes
2 shallots
1 tablespoon olive oil
1 ounce butter
1 bay leaf, or 2 basil leaves
salt and white pepper

Use this purée as the basis of other sauces, or as a garnish, or to fill mushrooms or other vegetables.

1. Blanch and peel **tomatoes,** core them, and chop them. Peel and mince **shallots.** Heat **oil** and **butter** in a large stainless-steel saucepan and sauté shallots until golden.
2. Add **tomatoes** and **bay leaf** or **basil leaves,** and cook over low heat, stirring often, until tomatoes are reduced to a soft purée. At that stage you may find it safer to set saucepan over an asbestos pad to prevent burning. Continue to cook until purée is thick.
3. Discard **bay leaf,** and put the whole mixture through a food mill. If **purée** is not as thick as you like it, return to a suacepan set over an asbestos pad and continue to cook, stirring often, until as thick as you like. Season with **salt** and **pepper** to taste.

variation: Lacking flavorful fresh tomatoes, this can be made with canned peeled plum tomatoes. Use three 20-ounce cans, drained; the drained tomato juice can be used for other recipes.
This purée can be frozen. Spoon it into 1-cup containers, allowing ample headspace, and cool, then freeze. Seal and label.

Raw Tomato Sauce

preparation time: 30 minutes
makes about 4 cups, enough
for 1 pound pasta

3 pounds very ripe tomatoes
6 shallots
10 parsley sprigs, including stems
4 fresh sage leaves, or 8 basil leaves, or 10 rosemary leaves
2 tablespoons olive oil
juice of 1/2 lemon
salt and pepper
2 ounces Romano cheese (optional)
2 ounces blue cheese (optional)

Use either plum tomatoes or round tomatoes for this sauce, but whichever you use, the tomatoes must be very ripe to get the full flavor. It is a delicious sauce for shellfish or vegetables but it is a special treat on pasta, particularly spinach pasta.

1. Blanch and peel **tomatoes,** core them, and cut into chunks. Peel and chop **shallots.** Wash **parsley** and roll in a towel to dry completely. Put **herb leaves** in a small strainer and pour boiling water over them. At once rinse with cold water and pat dry.
2. Combine **tomatoes, shallots, parsley** and **herbs,** and process them, about 2 cups at a time, in a food processor fitted with the steel blade. Put all the batches through a food mill to get rid of tomato seeds.
3. Combine all the batches and stir in **olive oil, lemon juice,** and **salt** and **pepper** to taste. Store at room temperature, covered, for several hours, or in the refrigerator overnight.
4. If sauce was refrigerated, bring to room temperature to serve.
5. For pasta, grate **Romano cheese** and toss with drained hot pasta, then pour about a third of the sauce over and toss again. Serve the rest of the sauce separately. Or crumble the **blue cheese,** stir it into tomato sauce, and toss part of it with pasta.

variation: Purée and strain only 2 pounds tomatoes. Dice the rest, discarding as many seeds as possible, and stir the dice into the purée to give a different texture.

53

Smooth Tomato Sauce

preparation time: 20 minutes
cooking time: 40 minutes
makes about 4 cups

4 pounds fresh tomatoes, preferably plum tomatoes
1 pound yellow onions
4 celery ribs with leaves
2 carrots
6 parsley sprigs
6 basil leaves
1/4 cup olive oil
1 cup water or chicken stock
salt and pepper
sugar or honey

1. Wash and core **tomatoes** and cut them into chunks. Peel and chop
onions. Wash and dry **celery,** and cut ribs and leaves into slices. Scrape and
chop **carrots.** Wash and dry **parsley** and **basil.**
2. Heat **olive oil** in a large heavy saucepan. Sauté **onions** until golden. Stir in
celery, carrots, parsley and **basil.** Cook for 1 minute. Finally add **tomatoes**
and the cup of **water** or **stock.**
3. Simmer the **sauce** over low heat, stirring often, for 30 minutes, or until
tomatoes are reduced to a lumpy purée. Purée the sauce, 2 cups at a time, in
a food processor or blender.
4. Return sauce to the pan and taste. Add **salt** if needed, a few grinds of
pepper, and **sugar** or **honey,** 1 to 3 teaspoons of either, if the acid needs to
be balanced. Heat sauce enough to dissolve salt and sugar.
5. Sauce can be frozen. Cool it, then pour into 2-cup freezer containers,
allowing 1 inch of headspace, and freeze. When frozen, seal and label.

variation: In wintertime, use 6 to 8 cups canned peeled whole tomatoes,
Italian-style plum tomatoes or American round tomatoes.
Other herbs can be used to change the taste balance. Try orégano, rosemary,
chile pepper flakes.

Chunky Tomato Sauce

1. Assemble the ingredients for **Smooth Tomato Sauce.** Set aside 2 pounds of the **tomatoes.** Blanch and peel these, cut into halves, and scoop out the center pulp and seeds. Add the scooped-out pulp to the rest of the tomatoes.

2. Make tomato sauce, following Steps 2 and 3. Meanwhile dice the peeled **tomatoes,** making pieces about the size of a large green pea.

3. Add **tomato dice** to puréed sauce and let sauce simmer for a few extra minutes, until dice are tender.

4. This sauce can also be frozen. This is delicious served on fish, veal, pasta.

Marinara Sauce

preparation time: 10 minutes
cooking time: 40 minutes
makes 2-1/2 to 3 cups

2 pounds fresh plum tomatoes
2 garlic cloves
1 onion, 3 ounces
1/4 cup olive oil
1 tablespoon minced fresh basil
4 tablespoons minced fresh parsley
salt and pepper
1 teaspoon minced fresh orégano

This simple quick sauce (mariner's sauce) is widely used in Southern Italy for pasta, risotto, fish fresh out of the water and other seafood.

1. Blanch and peel **tomatoes;** chop them. Peel **garlic.** Peel and chop **onion.**

2. Heat **olive oil** in a deep skillet or saucepan. Push **garlic** through a press into the pan and add **onion.** Sauté until onion is translucent.

3. Add tomatoes, **basil** and half of the **parsley.** Simmer, stirring often, for 20 to 30 minutes.

4. Season sauce with **salt** and **pepper.** Stir in the **orégano** and remaining parsley. Serve sauce while it is fresh and hot.

Tomato-Meat Sauce for Pasta

preparation time: 1 hour
cooking time: 2 to 3 hours
makes about 4 cups, enough
for 1-1/2 pounds pasta

1 ounce dried Italian mushrooms (porcini)
1 cup dry red wine
2 pounds fresh tomatoes
3 garlic cloves
1/2 pound yellow onions
4 sprigs of Italian parsley
1 pound boneless beef chuck or top round
3 tablespoons olive oil
1 teaspoon dried orégano
beef stock (optional)
salt and pepper

1. Soak the **mushrooms** in the **wine** for 20 to 30 minutes. Discard tough stems and slice the caps. Filter the soaking wine and set aside.
2. Blanch and peel **tomatoes,** core them, and chop them. Peel **garlic.** Peel and chop **onions.** Wash and dry **parsley** and cut into small bits. Chop the **beef;** do not grind it.
3. Heat **oil** in a heavy saucepan and in it brown the **garlic cloves.** Lift them out. (Garlic can be discarded at this point, or can be chopped and set aside to add later.) Add chopped **beef** to the saucepan and cook over low heat, stirring often, until meat loses its red color and begins to brown.
4. Add **onions** and **sliced mushrooms** and cook for about 5 minutes, stirring all the while. Add chopped **tomatoes, garlic** if you use it, **parsley, orégano** and the filtered **wine.** Mix all together and continue to cook for several hours. Set the pan over an asbestos pad to prevent burning. If the sauce seems to be sticking, add **beef stock,** 1/4 cup at a time. Do not let the sauce burn for that spoils the flavor.
5. When sauce reaches the texture you like, remove from heat and season with **salt** and freshly ground **pepper.**

variations: Use canned peeled plum tomatoes, two 20-ounce cans, when fresh tomatoes are not flavorful.
Beef chuck has some fat, top round very little. Choose whichever you prefer. However, so-called "hamburger" will not do as it makes the sauce too fatty, also less flavorful.

Red Clam Sauce

preparation time: 30 minutes
cooking time: 15 minutes
serves 6, enough sauce for 1
pound linguine

3 dozen small Little Neck clams
2 pounds ripe tomatoes
1 onion, 3 ounces
1 large garlic clove
1/4 cup olive oil
1/4 cup chopped parsley
black pepper

1. Scrub **clams.** They can be refrigerated for a few hours to make it easier to open them. Shuck clams, saving and straining all the juices, and refrigerate clams and juice separately. If opening them is too difficult, put clams in a steamer over 1-1/2 cups water or half water and half white wine, and steam for about 5 minutes, shaking the pan after 2 minutes to allow even steaming. Discard shells, and filter the liquid into a clean container.

2. Blanch and peel **tomatoes,** core them, and chop them. Peel and chop **onion.** Peel **garlic.**

3. Heat **olive oil** in a large saucepan and sauté **garlic** until golden. Discard garlic. Add **onion** and sauté until translucent. Add chopped **tomatoes** and simmer until tomatoes are very soft and somewhat reduced. Pour in reserved **clam juices** and cook for another 5 minutes.

4. Finally, drop in the **clams** and **parsley** and simmer the sauce only until well heated; do not cook the clams lest they toughen. Add **black pepper** to taste. Serve at once; this sauce is much less good if reheated, so eat it all at one go.

variation: When good fresh tomatoes are lacking, use canned peeled tomatoes, whatever variety you like; use two 20-ounce cans, but drain off some of the juice for other recipes.

Sauce Espagnole

preparation time: 20 minutes
cooking time: 6 hours, plus
time to make stock
makes 2-1/2 quarts

3/4 cup clarified butter
3/4 cup all-purpose flour
6 quarts unsalted brown stock
2 pounds fresh tomatoes
1/2 pound carrots
1/2 pound yellow onions
2 ounces prosciutto or other uncooked ham
1 bay leaf
salt and pepper

Why is this brown sauce called "espagnole"? Because of those tomatoes! French brown sauce was "improved" by the Spanish cooks who were attached to the train of Anne of Austria, daughter of Philip III of Spain, when she arrived in France to marry Louis XIII. Remember, the Spanish explorers brought the tomato to Europe. The credit for this is often wrongly given to Catherine de Médicis, the Italian princess who married Henri II.

1. Heat 1/2 cup of the **clarified butter** in an 8-quart stockpot and stir in the **flour.** Cook over very low heat, stirring all the while, until the roux is light brown and smells of hazelnuts.
2. Slowly pour in the **stock** and whisk over moderate heat, combining roux and stock, until the mixture comes to a boil. Set over low heat so that the sauce simmers, and continue this for 2 to 4 hours, until reduced to 4 quarts. (Did we say it was easy?) Skim the sauce all the while; that is the most important step.
3. Wash and core **tomatoes,** and chop. Scrub and chop **carrots.** Peel and chop **onions.** Mince **prosciutto.** Crumble **bay leaf.** Heat remaining **clarified butter** in a separate saucepan and in it sauté the chopped **carrots, onions, prosciutto** and crumbled **bay leaf** (this mixture is called a mirepoix).
4. When mirepoix is golden, add it and the **tomatoes** to the stockpot. Continue to simmer the sauce for 2 hours more, skimming often.
5. When reduced to 2-1/2 quarts, strain the **sauce** into a clean pan or a large bowl. Cool the sauce, stirring now and then to prevent formation of a skin.
6. Pour into 1-cup freezer jars and refrigerate or freeze. The sauce should be glossy and perfectly smooth. Season with **salt** and **pepper** when you are ready to use it. Use by itself or as a basis for other sauces.

Chili Sauce

preparation time: 1 hour
cooking time: 1 hour, or more
makes 8 to 10 pints

10 pounds fully ripe red tomatoes
1-1/2 pounds yellow onions
1-1/2 pounds green peppers
1 cup cider vinegar or white vinegar
6 tablespoons sugar
4 tablespoons sea salt or Kosher salt
3 cinnamon sticks
1 tablespoon whole cloves
1 teaspoon black peppercorns
1 teaspoon coriander berries

This is entirely different from commercial chili sauce, and the name is a mystery since there isn't a chile in it. In our family this was the favorite relish and we always finished every jar long before winter was over.

1. Blanch and peel the **tomatoes,** and core them. Chop them and put them in a large enamelware kettle, about 8-quart size. Peel and chop **onions** and add to tomatoes. Peel **peppers** with a swivel vegetable peeler, trim them, discard stems, ribs and seeds, and chop peppers. Add these also to the tomatoes.
2. Pour **vinegar, sugar** and **salt** into the vegetables and stir over low heat until sugar and salt are dissolved. Break up the **cinnamon sticks.** In a mortar crush **cloves, peppercorns** and **coriander berries.** Tie all the spices in a cheesecloth bag and add to the kettle.
3. Cook everything over low heat, stirring often with a wooden spoon, until the **pickle** reaches the consistency that suits you; allow at least 1 hour, but cook longer if necessary—the pickle should be rather thick. Discard the bag of spices.
4. Ladle hot pickle into sterilized 1-pint or 1-cup jars, seal, and set on a wooden rack to cool. Because of the sugar, salt, vinegar and natural acid in the tomatoes, we never found it necessary to process this; also we ate it up so fast. However, it can be processed like any other preserve, in hot-water bath or in pressure cooker. Or it can be frozen in 1-cup containers. This pickle is dark-colored because of the spices, not bright red. The taste is wonderful.

variation: If you like, you can increase the proportions of onions and peppers. After you have made a batch of this, you may want to adjust the amounts of seasoning and spices in future batches.

Green Tomato Marmalade

preparation time: 20 minutes
cooking time: about 1 hour
makes 7 or 8 glasses, 6-ounce
size

3 pounds green tomatoes
4 lemons
salt
4 ounces fresh gingerroot
4 cups sugar

This marmalade is not designed for morning toast; rather it is to be served as a relish with meat, especially poultry and lamb.

1. Wash **tomatoes** thoroughly; they will not be peeled for the marmalade. Set them on a rack or paper towels to dry.
2. With a vegetable peeler remove the yellow rind of the **lemons.** Put the pieces in a small saucepan, cover with cold water, add a pinch of **salt,** and bring to a boil. Boil for 2 minutes, drain, rinse, and repeat the whole procedure. Roll the lemon rind pieces in a paper towel to blot excess water, then drop the pieces into the bowl of a food processor fitted with the steel blade.
3. Peel the **gingerroot,** cut into chunks, and add to the **lemon rind.** Pour in 1 cup of the **sugar** and process until lemon rind and gingerroot are grated. Put the mixture into a large kettle.
4. Cut out the cores and blossom scars of the **tomatoes,** and cut them into 1-inch chunks. Drop them into the kettle. Squeeze the **juice** of the **lemons** and add to tomatoes. Finally pour in remaining **sugar** and add 1/2 teaspoon **salt.**
5. Over low heat stir the mixture until the **sugar** is completely dissolved. Then bring the marmalade to a boil and reduce heat to a steady simmer. Cook for about 1 hour, stirring often. Toward the end of the cooking, **marmalade** will become dark green, shiny and translucent. When it reaches that stage, be sure to stir often to prevent sticking.
6. While **marmalade** cooks, wash jelly glasses in hot soapy water, rinse well, then sterilize them. Drain upside down.
7. As soon as 2 drops of the syrup run together on the edge of a large spoon, turn off the heat and spoon **marmalade** into glasses. Let them stand on a wooden board or rack, not on a porcelain or metal surface. Use a moistened paper towel to clean the rim of the glasses, then pour in melted paraffin to cover marmalade. When glasses are cooled, cover them with the metal covers, or wrap in aluminum foil.

Green Tomato and Apple Marmalade

preparation time: 20 minutes,
plus 36 hours for soaking
cooking time: 40 to 50 minutes
makes about 8 glasses,
6-ounce size, or 4 jars,
1-1/2 cup size

2 pounds green tomatoes
2 pounds cooking apples
2 pounds sugar
1/4 cup lemon juice
1/4 cup water
12 whole cloves
2 cinnamon sticks
1 teaspoon salt

1. Wash the **tomatoes** carefully. Remove cores and blossom scars. Cut tomatoes across into halves and cut each half into thin little wedges. Drop the pieces into a large pottery bowl. Wash and peel the **apples,** core them, and cut into 1-inch chunks. Add to tomatoes.

2. Pour in **sugar, lemon juice** and **water.** Mix with a wooden spoon and let the mixture stand at room temperature, stirring now and then, for 36 hours.

3. Turn the syrupy mixture into a kettle. Add **cloves, cinnamon** and **salt.** Bring to a boil and simmer for 40 to 50 minutes, until apple chunks are translucent. Do not keep cooking until the syrup sheets off a spoon, as the mixture may start to burn on the bottom. It should be very shiny and syrupy looking. Discard **cinnamon sticks; cloves** can remain, but try to distribute them among the jars.

4. Spoon into sterilized jelly jars or preserve jars. Let them stand on a wooden board or rack, not on a porcelain or metal surface. Use a moistened paper towel to clean the rim of the glasses, then pour in melted paraffin to cover marmalade. When jars are cool, cover with metal covers, or glass preserve tops, or wrap in aluminum foil.

5. Let this mature for a few weeks before using it. While it is not a marmalade, as it lacks any citrus fruit, the apple pieces give it a marmalade texture.

Spicy Sour Green Tomato Pickles

preparation time: about 1 hour,
plus 12 hours for salting
tomatoes
cooking time: about 1 hour
makes 5 to 6 pints

4 pounds green tomatoes

1-1/2 tablespoons sea salt or Kosher salt

2 pounds onions

4 large red bell peppers

4 fresh hot red peppers

2 quarts cider vinegar

1/2 tablespoon black peppercorns

1 tablespoon coriander berries

2 tablespoons mustard seeds

4 cinnamon sticks, broken

1. Wash **tomatoes** carefully and drain. Core them, and cut them into small wedges. Layer them in a large bowl, sprinkling each layer with some of the **salt.** (Do not use ordinary table salt, as the additional ingredients interfere with pickling.) Let the bowl of tomatoes sit overnight in a cool place, not the refrigerator.

2. Next day, drain off the liquid accumulated around the **tomatoes.** Peel and slice **onions.**

3. Use a vegetable peeler to remove skin from the **red bell peppers;** or, if you prefer, roast these peppers in the oven or broiler until the skin is charred, then remove the skin. Also remove stems, ribs and seeds. Cut peppers into squares or slivers.

4. Wear plastic or rubber gloves to work with the **hot peppers.** Cut off stem ends, slit peppers, and rinse off seeds. Cut these into small squares or slivers and mix with the bell pepper pieces. Wash gloves before removing them.

5. Empty 1 quart of **vinegar** into a stainless-steel or enamelware saucepan and add all the **spices.** Bring to a boil and boil for about 30 minutes. Cool, then pour through a fine strainer into a container with a pouring spout and add the second quart of vinegar.

6. Use an enamelware kettle (the lower pan of a blanching kettle is a good size for this amount of ingredients). Put the ingredients in the kettle, first some **tomatoes,** then some **onions,** then some of the **red peppers,** then pour in some **vinegar.** Continue until everything is used.

7. Slowly bring the mixture to a boil and simmer until all the vegetables are tender, but not mushy.

8. Ladle the **pickles** into sterilized preserving jars, and pour in enough of the vinegar to cover the vegetables. Seal the jars, and store in a cool place.

9. These pickles, chopped, make an excellent addition to sandwich fillings; also good mixed into seafood salads—plain tuna becomes special with this addition. Serve with other relishes for "sweets and sours." The vinegar can be added to sauces or salad dressings for a flavor fillip.

Tomato and Herb Vinegar

preparation time: 10 minutes, plus 2 days to mellow
makes 1 1/2 cups

1/2 pound very ripe tomatoes
1 cup white-wine vinegar
3 tablespoons minced fresh celery leaves
2 tablespoons minced dill leaves
1 teaspoon fennel seeds
1 garlic clove

Use this for salad dressings, vegetables vinaigrette, sweet-and-sour mixtures, and to give an unusual taste to chicken cooked with vinegar.

1. Wash **tomatoes,** core them, and remove blossom scars. Cut into chunks and drop into the container of an electric blender or the bowl of a food processor fitted with the steel blade. Pour in the **vinegar** and process until tomatoes are puréed in the vinegar.
2. Add **celery** and **dill leaves** and process for another second. Pour into a jar with a cover. Crush **fennel seeds** in a mortar and add. Peel **garlic** and drop it whole into the jar. Stir or shake to mix well.
3. Store the vinegar in refrigerator for 2 days to mellow.
4. Pour vinegar through a coarse strainer into a clean jar, pressing hard against the solids to release as much of the liquid as possible. Then pour through a fine strainer into a bottle. Continue to keep in refrigerator, and use within a week.

variation: For long-keeping vinegar, bring to a boil and simmer for 5 minutes before adding fennel and garlic. Dried celery and dried dill can be used in place of fresh; use half as much dried.

63

Index